NFL TODAY

THE STORY OF THE

BALTIMORE RAVENS

NFL TODAY

THE STORY OF THE BALTIMORE RAVENS

SARA GILBERT

CREATIVE EDUCATION

PUBLISHED BY CREATIVE EDUCATION
P.O. BOX 227, MANKATO, MINNESOTA 56002
CREATIVE EDUCATION IS AN IMPRINT OF THE CREATIVE COMPANY
WWW.THECREATIVECOMPANY.US

DESIGN AND PRODUCTION BY BLUE DESIGN
ART DIRECTION BY RITA MARSHALL
PRINTED IN THE UNITED STATES OF AMERICA

PHOTOGRAPHS BY CORBIS (REUTERS), GETTY IMAGES
(JUSTIN K. ALLER, NEIL BRAKE/AFP, SIMON BRUTY/
SPORTS ILLUSTRATED, TIMOTHY A. CLARK/AFP,
JAMES DRAKE/SPORTS ILLUSTRATED, G. FLUME,
FOCUS ON SPORT, LARRY FRENCH, OTTO GREULE
JR., TOM HAUCK/ALLSPORT, DOUG KAPUSTIN/
MCT, ANDY LYONS/ALLSPORT, DAVID MAXWELL, AL
MESSERSCHMIDT, DOUG PENSINGER/ALLSPORT, TOM
PIDGEON/ALLSPORT, TIM SLOAN/AFP, PATRICK SMITH,
MATT SULLIVAN, GENE SWEENY JR./BALTIMORE
SUN/MCT, KEVIN TERRELL, AL TIELEMANS/
SPORTS ILLUSTRATED, TRAVEL INK, ROB TRINGALI/
SPORTSCHROME, GEORGE TROTT, DILIP VISHWANAT,
NICK WASS)

LIBRARY OF CONGRESS CATALOGING-IN-PUBLICATION DATA
GILBERT, SARA.
THE STORY OF THE BALTIMORE RAVENS / SARA GILBERT.
P. CM. — (NFL TODAY)
INCLUDES INDEX.
SUMMARY: THE HISTORY OF THE NATIONAL FOOTBALL LEAGUE'S
BALTIMORE RAVENS, SURVEYING THE FRANCHISE'S BIGGEST
STARS AND MOSTMEMORABLE MOMENTS FROM ITS INAUGURAL
SEASON IN 1996 TO TODAY.
ISBN 978-1-60818-294-7
1. BALTIMORE RAVENS (FOOTBALL TEAM)—HISTORY—JUVENILE
LITERATURE. I. TITLE.

GV956.B3G44 2013
796.332'640975271—DC23   2012027215

FIRST EDITION
9 8 7 6 5 4 3 2 1

COVER: QUARTERBACK JOE FLACCO
PAGE 2: WIDE RECEIVER ANQUAN BOLDIN
PAGES 4-5: DEFENSIVE TACKLE MA'AKE KEMOEATU
PAGE 6: OFFENSIVE LINEMAN MARSHALL YANDA

TABLE OF CONTENTS

A KEY SEAPORT, BALTIMORE IS FAMED FOR ITS SHIPBUILDING

Battles in Baltimore

Baltimore, Maryland, has a long history of celebrating important victories. In 1814, American soldiers stationed at Fort McHenry had to defend the city against an attack by the powerful and well-armed British navy in one of the most critical battles of the War of 1812. British bombs exploded in Baltimore's harbor all night long, and many residents feared that their city would be captured by the time morning came. But when dawn broke, the American flag was still flying at Fort McHenry, the British were retreating, and a young lawyer named Francis Scott Key was penning a poem about the battle. That poem became known as "The Star Spangled Banner," and in 1931 it was officially adopted as the national anthem of the United States.

Starting in 1953, that anthem was played before battles of a different sort in Baltimore. For 30 years, the Baltimore Colts fought against opponents in the National Football League (NFL) to bring a championship trophy to the city. The Colts collected three NFL championships for their dedicated fans before owner Robert Irsay moved the

THE RAVENS WERE INSTANTLY TOUGH, THANKS TO STARS SUCH AS RAY LEWIS

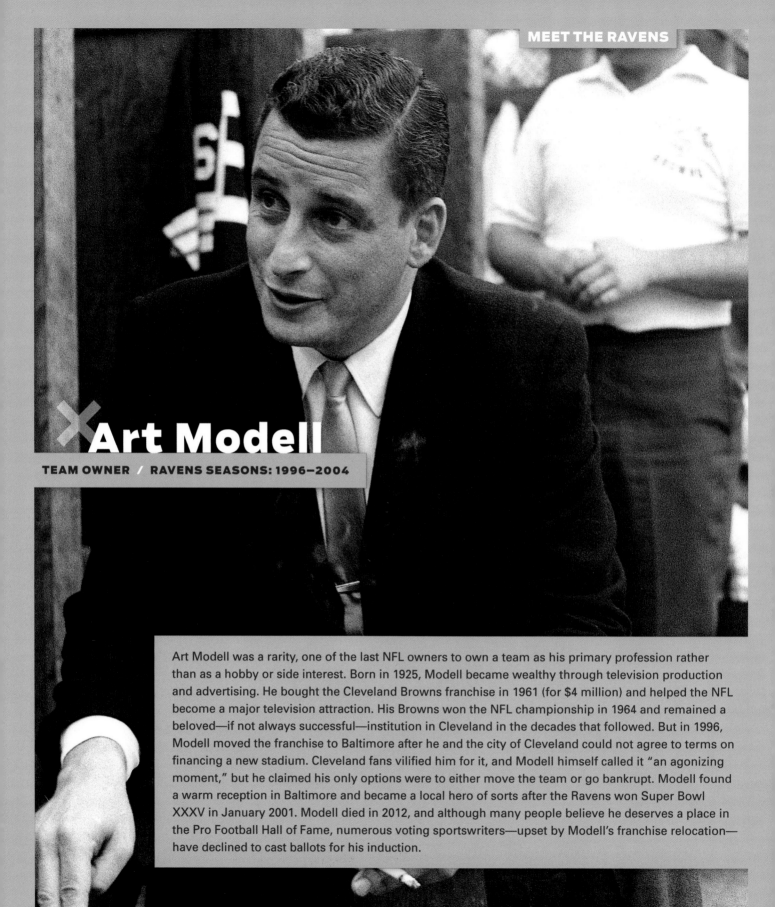

Art Modell

TEAM OWNER / RAVENS SEASONS: 1996—2004

Art Modell was a rarity, one of the last NFL owners to own a team as his primary profession rather than as a hobby or side interest. Born in 1925, Modell became wealthy through television production and advertising. He bought the Cleveland Browns franchise in 1961 (for $4 million) and helped the NFL become a major television attraction. His Browns won the NFL championship in 1964 and remained a beloved—if not always successful—institution in Cleveland in the decades that followed. But in 1996, Modell moved the franchise to Baltimore after he and the city of Cleveland could not agree to terms on financing a new stadium. Cleveland fans vilified him for it, and Modell himself called it "an agonizing moment," but he claimed his only options were to either move the team or go bankrupt. Modell found a warm reception in Baltimore and became a local hero of sorts after the Ravens won Super Bowl XXXV in January 2001. Modell died in 2012, and although many people believe he deserves a place in the Pro Football Hall of Fame, numerous voting sportswriters—upset by Modell's franchise relocation—have declined to cast ballots for his induction.

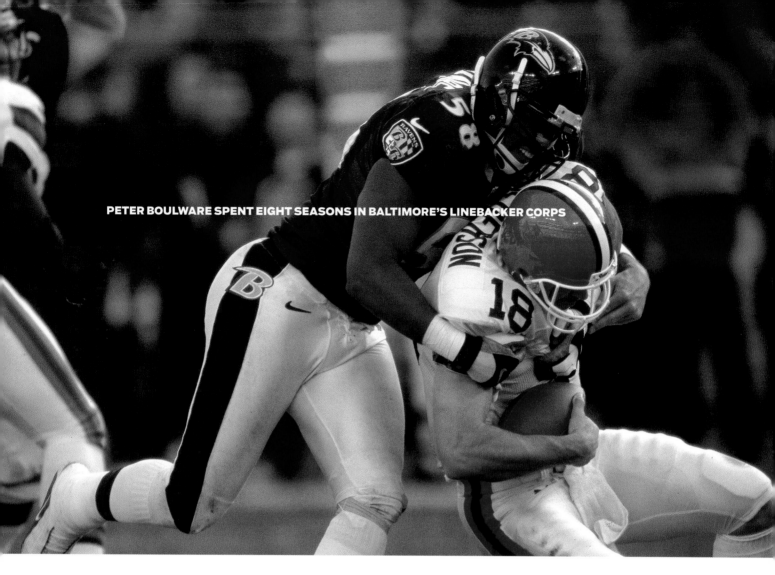

PETER BOULWARE SPENT EIGHT SEASONS IN BALTIMORE'S LINEBACKER CORPS

team to Indianapolis, Indiana, in 1984. Even then, the city kept fighting, this time to bring another NFL team to town. Finally, in 1995, the owner of the Cleveland Browns announced that his team would move to Baltimore and begin playing there in 1996.

One of the reasons the Colts had left Baltimore was that they didn't like playing in the old and outdated Memorial Stadium. The Browns left Cleveland for the same reason, abandoning the aging Cleveland Municipal Stadium for a new home that Baltimore had promised to build for the team. But a new stadium wasn't all they needed. Owner Art Modell had agreed to let Cleveland keep the Browns name, colors, and official team records, which meant Baltimore had to create a new identity for its new team.

A Baltimore newspaper asked the city's residents to suggest names for the team. Many of the popular choices played on the city's importance to U.S. history, with entries such as "Americans" and "Marauders." The winning suggestion, however, was taken from a famous poem written in Baltimore by Edgar Allan Poe in the 1840s: the Ravens, after the black, talking bird that torments a broken-hearted man in Poe's poem "The Raven."

"We took our share of lumps."

TED MARCHIBRODA

After a name was established, the Ravens needed a coach. Modell hired Ted Marchibroda, who had coached the old Baltimore Colts from 1975 to 1979, to turn around a team that had finished 5–11 in its final season in Cleveland. The veteran coach knew he could build the offense around quarterback Vinny Testaverde and the defense around hard-hitting safety Stevon Moore—but he also knew he needed young talent to give the Ravens a chance in the American Football Conference (AFC) Central Division, which was frequently dominated by the Pittsburgh Steelers.

In the 1996 NFL Draft, the Ravens selected giant offensive tackle Jonathan Ogden and ferocious middle linebacker Ray Lewis. The 6-foot-9 and 340-pound Ogden was known for his enormous strength, quick feet, and keen understanding of the game. Lewis was a tough tackler whose confidence added swagger to the defense.

The Ravens won their home opener 19–14 over the Oakland Raiders in front of 64,000 fans in Memorial Stadium, where the team would play its first two seasons. Ogden and Lewis were key components both in that victory and throughout the season. Lewis made a team-leading 95 tackles, and Ogden's barricading protection allowed Testaverde to throw for 4,177 yards—including 429 in a single game against the St. Louis Rams—and 33 touchdown passes. Despite its best efforts, however, Baltimore won only four games in 1996. "We took our share of lumps this year," said Coach Marchibroda. "But we had a lot of young players do a lot of growing up. We'll get better."

The team's defense needed the most improvement. In the 1997 NFL Draft, the team addressed that shortcoming by selecting nimble linebackers Peter Boulware and Jamie Sharper. Baltimore also signed huge defensive tackle Tony "The Goose" Siragusa. Although his barrel-shaped body seemed ill-matched to professional football, Siragusa's bulldozing playing style and colorful personality charmed the fans.

After improving to 6–9–1 in 1997, Baltimore drafted quick rookie cornerback Duane Starks and added experienced leadership to its core of young talent by signing crafty defensive back Rod Woodson in 1998. Along with these new players, the 1998 Ravens also had a new home: the beautiful new Ravens

Stars, Stallions, and Bombers

From 1953 to 1983, Baltimore was a thriving football town, the proud home of the three-time NFL champion Baltimore Colts. When the Colts moved to Indianapolis in 1984, fans were crushed. In the decade that followed, Baltimore was represented by two football teams in minor pro leagues—the Stars of the United States Football League (USFL) and the Stallions of the Canadian Football League (CFL), both of which won league championships—but it wasn't the same. In 1989, the NFL announced that it would be expanding by two franchises for the 1995 season. Officials in Baltimore launched an effort to land one of the franchises, going so far as to determine a team name—the Bombers—and develop a logo, which featured a military aircraft over a gold sunburst that resembled an explosion. Baltimore was one of five cities narrowed down as finalists, but in the end, the expansion franchises went to Charlotte, North Carolina, and Jacksonville, Florida, instead. When Baltimore finally got its team with the 1996 relocation of the Cleveland Browns, the shield-like logo of the Bombers was incorporated into the design of the original Ravens logo.

QUARTERBACK LEGEND JOHNNY UNITAS WAS THE FACE OF THE BALTIMORE COLTS

JERMAINE LEWIS NOTCHED SIX CAREER TOUCHDOWNS ON PUNT RETURNS

Stadium at Camden Yards in downtown Baltimore (which was renamed PSINet Stadium in January 1999 and later became M&T Bank Stadium).

Unfortunately, the thrill of the new stadium did not improve the Ravens' fortunes. The defense was solid, and 5-foot-7 receiver Jermaine Lewis emerged as one of the most electrifying kick returners in the league. But when the offense sputtered, the team stumbled to a 6–10 finish. The biggest highlight of the year occurred late in the season when the Colts returned to town. The Ravens fell behind but surged back with 25 points in the second half to beat Indianapolis in a 38–31 shoot-out. Disappointed with the team's overall lack of progress, though, Baltimore fired Coach Marchibroda after the season.

Jonathan Ogden

OFFENSIVE TACKLE / RAVENS SEASONS: 1996–2007 / HEIGHT: 6-FOOT-9 / WEIGHT: 340 POUNDS

Jonathan Ogden was a mountain of a man, even by NFL standards. Although his size and power were obvious, what made him unique were his nimble feet and intelligent approach to the game. Like most great offensive linemen, Ogden toiled in relative obscurity. Since the only time a spotlight shines on an offensive lineman during a game is when he commits a penalty or is beaten on a play, Ogden received little fanfare. Yet the Ravens recognized how special he was, rewarding him in 2000 with a $44-million contract, at the time the largest in league history for an offensive lineman. Opponents thought highly of Ogden as well. "You have to try to keep him off-balance, but he is so big and his arms are so big that it is hard to do," said New York Giants defensive end Cedric Jones. "I bet you could put him anywhere on the field and he would do all right." The future Hall-of-Famer always seemed to make the most of the opportunities given to him, catching two career passes ... for two total yards and two touchdowns.

The Men in the Middle

Many football historians regard the 2000 Ravens as the best defensive team in NFL history. The statistics certainly support that conclusion, as that Ravens squad surrendered the meager averages of 10.3 points and 60.6 rushing yards per game—both league records. And even though the team's great linebackers received most of the accolades, the players most responsible for the success of that season and the 2001 campaign might have been massive defensive tackles Sam Adams and Tony Siragusa. Although slow, their bulk (nearly 350 pounds each) and power enabled Adams and Siragusa to either devour running backs who ran up the middle or draw double-team blocking, meaning that players such as Ray Lewis could make tackles while facing few blockers. "We won the Super Bowl in 2000," Lewis later acknowledged, "because we had two guys in front of me that told me, 'You will not be touched.'" The Ravens' defense slipped a bit after Adams and "The Goose" left town in 2002, but in 2006, Baltimore tried to return to its winning formula by drafting another huge run-stuffer, defensive tackle Haloti Ngata.

ALMOST IMMOVABLE, TONY SIRAGUSA ANCHORED A STOUT RAVENS DEFENSE

Soaring to the Super Bowl

The Ravens' point-scoring woes led them to hire Brian Billick, an offense-minded coach, in 1999. During his seven years as offensive coordinator for the Minnesota Vikings, Billick had put together one of the most fearsome offenses the NFL had ever seen. During the 1998 season, Minnesota had scored an NFL-record 556 points—including 38 points in a lopsided victory over the Ravens. "We had identified Brian as one of the top young coaches in the game," said Art Modell. "But after that performance, we became convinced that he would be our top choice."

Billick knew that the Ravens' defense was among the best in the league. With Lewis, Boulware, and Sharper as linebackers, Siragusa anchoring a defensive line that included ends Rob Burnett and Michael McCrary, and speedy defensive backs such

ALTHOUGH NEVER A STAR, TRENT DILFER FOUND SUPER BOWL GLORY IN BALTIMORE

Ray Lewis

LINEBACKER / RAVENS SEASONS: 1996–2012 / HEIGHT: 6-FOOT-1 / WEIGHT: 245 POUNDS

Dick Butkus. Lawrence Taylor. Ray Lewis. Such is the reputation of Ray Lewis that any discussion of the greatest linebackers in NFL history must include "Ray-Ray." Number 52 had it all: great instincts, good speed, and vicious hitting power. As Miami Dolphins general manager Randy Mueller said, "He wants to break someone in half each time he hits them." Lewis's ability was made evident by the slew of awards won during his career—2 NFL Defensive Player of the Year awards (2000 and 2003), a Super Bowl Most Valuable Player (MVP) award, and 13 Pro Bowl selections. But what truly elevated him into the realm of all-time greats was the passion and vocal leadership he brought onto the field. Fellow Ravens defenders played with an extra bit of energy for fear of letting Lewis down. Lewis's legacy was tarnished somewhat in February 2000, when he was charged with murder after two men were killed outside an Atlanta nightclub during a Super Bowl party. He was ultimately cleared of the most serious charges and came back to lead his team to victory in the Super Bowl a year later.

"He wants to break someone in half."

MIAMI DOLPHINS GENERAL MANAGER
RANDY MUELLER ON RAY LEWIS

as Woodson, Starks, and cornerback Chris McAllister, the Ravens could put a stranglehold on opposing offenses. But with the exception of Ogden, Baltimore's offense had just mediocre ability.

Billick loved coordinating offenses that featured high-powered passing attacks. But in Baltimore, he didn't have the type of talent needed to run an explosive offense through the air. Instead, he installed a low-risk, run-oriented offense, choosing to play conservatively with the ball and rely on his fierce defense to hold opponents down.

The Ravens started the 1999 season 3–6. But then the team took flight, averaging 26 points per game the rest of the year. Much of the offensive spark came when backup quarterback Tony Banks stepped in at midseason and tossed 17 touchdown passes—many of them to receiver Qadry Ismail, a speedster who piled up more than 1,000 receiving yards. Behind these efforts and those of the NFL's second-best defense, Baltimore won five of its last seven games to finish 8–8. "We've built a little fire here," said Coach Billick. "It will be interesting to see how big it gets."

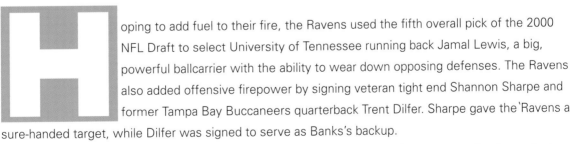

Hoping to add fuel to their fire, the Ravens used the fifth overall pick of the 2000 NFL Draft to select University of Tennessee running back Jamal Lewis, a big, powerful ballcarrier with the ability to wear down opposing defenses. The Ravens also added offensive firepower by signing veteran tight end Shannon Sharpe and former Tampa Bay Buccaneers quarterback Trent Dilfer. Sharpe gave the Ravens a sure-handed target, while Dilfer was signed to serve as Banks's backup.

The Ravens soared to a 5–1 start in 2000. The fearsome defense led the way, not allowing a single point in three of those six games. But the Ravens' offense, which had looked so promising at the end of the previous season, got worse in 2000. Banks's performance was marked by interceptions, fumbles,

Thirty-Six Super Seconds

Super Bowl XXXV, after the 2000 season, was a defensive showcase, as Baltimore gave up just 152 yards of offense and crushed the New York Giants 34–7. But that championship game is also remembered for 36 seconds that have been called the most exciting in Super Bowl history. The drama started late in the third quarter, when Ravens cornerback Duane Starks intercepted a pass by Giants quarterback Kerry Collins and returned it 49 yards for a touchdown. On the ensuing kickoff, Giants kick returner Ron Dixon eluded the Ravens' coverage team and took the ball the length of the field for New York's only score of the game. Then the Ravens returned the favor. Small and shifty kick returner Jermaine Lewis fielded the kickoff and wove his way over 84 yards of turf for a touchdown of his own. In 3 plays, 21 total points were put on the scoreboard—the fastest scoring flurry in Super Bowl history. "When we ran back our kick," said Baltimore coach Brian Billick, "it fueled us. And you could see the air go out of [the Giants]."

JERMAINE LEWIS'S KICK RETURN SCORE WAS THE SEVENTH IN SUPER BOWL HISTORY

TALKATIVE END SHANNON SHARPE WOULD LATER BECOME A TELEVISION ANALYST

and inaccuracy as the Ravens went four straight games without scoring an offensive touchdown.

Billick inserted Dilfer as the starting quarterback in the season's second half. The decision paid off, as Dilfer led the Ravens to seven straight victories. Dilfer was a solid field general, and Jamal Lewis rumbled for 1,364 rushing yards, but it was the Baltimore defense that made headlines. Ray Lewis and his fellow defenders surrendered only 165 total points—an NFL record for a 16-game season. This phenomenal effort carried the Ravens to a 12–4 record and their first playoff berth. "We're no offensive juggernaut," said Sharpe. "But we don't have to be. If we score 17 points, Ray and the 'D' will make it stick."

Sharpe's words seemed prophetic when the Ravens advanced to Super Bowl XXXV by allowing only 16 total points to the Denver Broncos, Tennessee Titans, and Oakland Raiders in the playoffs. In the Super Bowl, Baltimore faced a New York Giants team that had thrashed Minnesota 41–0 in its previous playoff game. But the Ravens could not be stopped. Dilfer hit receiver Brandon Stokley with a

ROB BURNETT POSTED 10.5 SACKS DURING THE 2000 SEASON

touchdown pass in the first quarter, Jermaine Lewis returned a kickoff 84 yards in the third quarter, and the Ravens' defense made 4 interceptions in Baltimore's 34–7 victory. Only a kick return for a touchdown kept the Giants from being shut out.

The Ravens shuffled their offensive lineup the next season, drafting talented tight end Todd Heap and signing former Kansas City Chiefs quarterback Elvis Grbac, who was considered a more polished passer, to take over for Dilfer. But the Ravens were dealt a serious blow when Jamal Lewis suffered a season-ending knee injury during training camp.

Despite the loss of their top running back, the Ravens put together a strong 10–6 season, beating the Vikings in the final game of the year to qualify for the playoffs. Hopes of a Super Bowl repeat ran high after Baltimore squashed the Miami Dolphins 20–3 in a first-round showdown. The win was a historic one, as it made the Ravens the first NFL team ever to win its first five playoff games. There would be no sixth straight win, though. The Ravens lost the next week, 27–10, to the rival Steelers.

Kicking Around

Much of the Ravens' success over the years has been attributed to the strength of its defense—but even defense can't win games without a little help. Between 1996 and 2008 in Baltimore, that help often came from one man: kicker Matt Stover. Stover scored 1,464 total points for the Ravens, including a career-high 135 in 2000. During that Super Bowl season, the team didn't score a single offensive touchdown for five consecutive games; Stover was personally responsible for all 42 points that the Ravens put up on the board during that time. Stover was so reliable that defensive players were once overheard begging coach Brian Billick to send Stover in to kick a field goal instead of letting the offense try for a touchdown. He was also so accurate that he raised expectations for all kickers. "Matt set the bar around 85 percent," said Ravens coach John Harbaugh. "Now that's what everybody wants. If you're not over 80 percent, you're not kicking in this league." The 2,004 points that Stover accumulated during his 19-year career ranked fourth all-time in the NFL when he retired in 2011.

MATT STOVER MADE THE ONLY PRO BOWL APPEARANCE OF HIS CAREER IN 2000

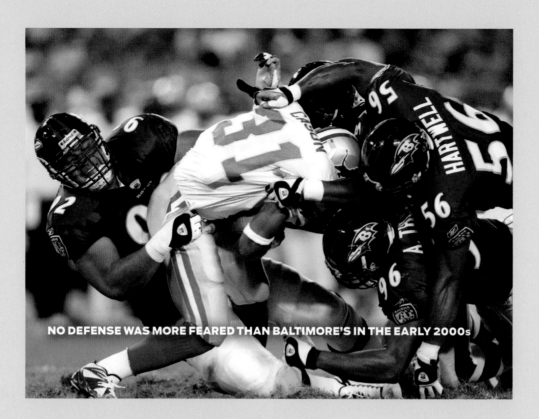

NO DEFENSE WAS MORE FEARED THAN BALTIMORE'S IN THE EARLY 2000s

Rebuilding in Baltimore

Baltimore found itself starting over in 2002. Sharpe and Woodson left town, Grbac retired, and Ray Lewis suffered a separated shoulder that sidelined him for most of the season. Veteran quarterback Jeff Blake and youngster Chris Redman ran the offense, and rookie safety Ed Reed took on a starting role, but the 2002 Ravens faded to 7–9.

In the 2003 NFL Draft, the Ravens reinforced their lineup by selecting pass-rushing linebacker Terrell Suggs and quarterback Kyle Boller. Suggs had set a national collegiate record with 24 quarterback sacks during his final season at Arizona State University, while Boller impressed team coaches in training camp with his powerful throwing arm and earned the starting job as a rookie.

Baltimore's quarterback play remained shaky in 2003 as Boller was injured and replaced by Anthony Wright. The good news, though, was that the rest of the team began to resemble its old Super Bowl–caliber self. Jamal Lewis had the season of a lifetime, rushing for an incredible 2,066 yards—the second-highest total in NFL history

SPEEDY TERRELL SUGGS WAS ONE OF THE NFL'S FIERCEST PASS RUSHERS

Brian Billick

COACH / RAVENS SEASONS: 1999–2007

Brian Billick was sometimes accused of being arrogant, a personality trait he did not deny. "If being arrogant is having self-confidence," he once said, "then I'm arrogant." That self-confidence—along with a willingness to adapt—helped Billick rise to the top of the NFL. When he was named the Ravens' head coach in 1999, Baltimore was going into its fourth season, having posted losing records its first three. Less than two years later, the Ravens were Super Bowl champions, and they returned to the grand stage of the NFL playoffs in two of the three seasons after that. Billick, who had spent time playing both linebacker and tight end in college, earned his coaching chance in Baltimore because of his offensive genius. But, perhaps surprisingly, he ended up building a team known for its ferocious, record-setting defense. His players in Baltimore appreciated his direct and assured leadership style. "More than any coach I played for, Brian treated the players with respect and got the most out of us," said star safety Rod Woodson. "He always got to the heart of things, no bull."

JAMAL LEWIS SCORED 14 TIMES DURING HIS BRILLIANT 2003 SEASON

to that point. Ray Lewis was healthy again and back to his dominant ways, winning his second NFL Defensive Player of the Year award. Suggs racked up 12 sacks to win the Defensive Rookie of the Year award, and linebacker Adalius Thomas emerged as a star with his aggressive special-teams tackling. These efforts helped the Ravens win their first AFC North Division championship (the NFL's divisions had been realigned in 2002) with a 10–6 record, but the season ended bitterly with a 20–17 loss to the Titans in the playoffs.

The 2004 season kicked off with a new team owner in Baltimore. Art Modell, who was then 78 years old, had sold majority ownership of the team to Baltimore businessman Steve Bisciotti in April 2004. Unfortunately, after paying the $600-million asking price, Bisciotti watched an unfortunate scene unfold in Baltimore. While the defense—led by the passionate play of Ray Lewis, Reed, Thomas, and veteran cornerback Deion Sanders—remained one of the NFL's scariest, the Ravens' offense bordered on inept. Jamal Lewis managed just 1,006 yards on the year, and Travis Taylor led all Ravens receivers with a meager 421 yards. Injuries compounded Baltimore's troubles, and the Ravens finished the year 9–7 and out of the playoffs. The outcome left the players disappointed. "It's disheartening to think that we're going to be one of those teams that's watching everyone else play in January," Ravens defensive end Marques Douglas said. "We want to be one of those elite teams, and this year, we're not."

The woes of 2004—a feeble offensive attack and injuries to key players—repeated themselves in 2005. Neither Wright nor Boller could get the offense in gear, and Jamal Lewis struggled after an off-season that included knee surgery and a four-month prison sentence on drug charges. The Ravens went

0–8 on the road and mustered just a 6–10 record overall.

Although 2005 ended with Baltimore's worst record in seven years, there were signs that a turnaround was on the horizon. Late in the season, the Ravens had beaten their rivals, the Steelers, 16–13, and obliterated the Green Bay Packers 48–3. After the season, the team made a move to improve its long-struggling quarterback play, signing veteran passer Steve McNair from the Titans. Although McNair was on the downside of his career, he was a former league MVP known for his toughness. Billick believed that with McNair throwing the ball to such up-and-coming receivers as Mark Clayton, the Ravens' offense might at last come close to matching the strength of its defense. McNair agreed. "I think this is a place we can win Super Bowls," he said. "That is the missing piece out of my career."

DEFENSIVE TACKLE MA'AKE KEMOEATU (LEFT) AND LINEBACKER TOMMY POLLEY

Ozzie's Wizardry

As a star tight end for the Cleveland Browns in the 1980s, Ozzie Newsome set an NFL record with 662 career pass receptions (a mark later broken by Ravens tight end Shannon Sharpe) and became known as the "Wizard of Oz." But Newsome's nickname seemed most appropriate after his playing days were over, when he became the "man behind the curtain" for the Ravens. As Baltimore's vice president of player personnel (starting in 1996) and then as its general manager (starting in 2002), Newsome was the brain behind the Ravens' NFL Draft selections and free-agent signings, and he was widely regarded as a genius at recognizing and obtaining talent. He was credited with building the roster that won Super Bowl XXXV, and over the course of a decade, he put such stars as Ray Lewis, Jonathan Ogden, Jamal Lewis, Todd Heap, and Ed Reed in Ravens purple. In 2005, *Sports Illustrated* writer Don Banks identified Newsome as the league's sharpest personnel mind, writing that "the Ravens are the NFL's gold standard on draft day, consistently making choices that stand the test of time."

OZZIE NEWSOME (LEFT) INTRODUCING THE SIGNING OF SHANNON SHARPE

SCRAPPY RECEIVER MARK CLAYTON HELPED DIVERSIFY THE RAVENS' OFFENSE

McNair's calm leadership and willingness to play through pain seemed to inspire his teammates in 2006. The Ravens started the season with a four-game winning streak and ended it with four straight wins for a 13–3 record and another AFC North title. The defense, featuring such newcomers as big rookie defensive tackle Haloti Ngata and veteran end Trevor Pryce, was resilient in the playoffs against the high-powered Indianapolis Colts, surrendering five field goals but no touchdowns. Unfortunately, McNair threw two interceptions, Heap lost a critical fumble, and Baltimore fell by a score of 15–6.

The Ravens let Jamal Lewis leave town after the season and replaced him with former Buffalo Bills halfback Willis McGahee. A versatile runner just entering the prime of his career, the 26-year-old McGahee had averaged 1,122 yards a year in his 3 seasons in Buffalo, and he galloped for 1,207 in a Ravens jersey in 2007. Unfortunately, he was one of the only bright spots in the most disappointing season in team history. The Ravens started out 4–2 but then collapsed, losing nine games in a row. The most embarrassing defeat came at the hands of the Miami Dolphins, who were 0–13 before beating the Ravens 22–16. McNair struggled before he was benched late in the season and replaced by Boller, and the once-impenetrable defense surrendered at least 27 points in 8 games. The dramatic drop-off prompted Bisciotti to fire Coach Billick the day after the season ended.

IN 2006, THE RAVENS AGAIN BOASTED THE TOP-RANKED DEFENSE IN THE LEAGUE

34

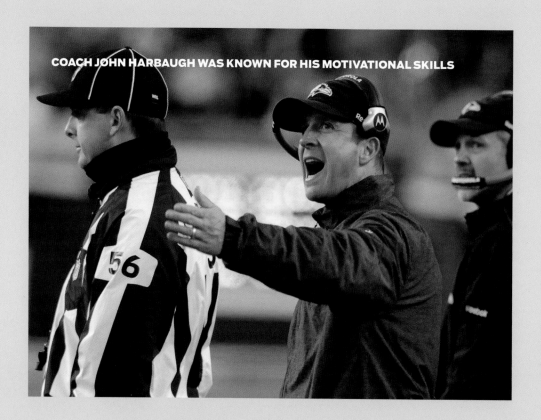

COACH JOHN HARBAUGH WAS KNOWN FOR HIS MOTIVATIONAL SKILLS

Handoff to Harbaugh

Hired as Billick's replacement was John Harbaugh, who had spent the previous 10 seasons as an assistant coach with the Philadelphia Eagles. Harbaugh inherited a team that he believed could quickly climb back to its place among the AFC's elite—and he was right. Although Ray Lewis was entering the twilight of his career, his inspirational leadership and the outstanding play of Reed, Suggs, and linebacker Bart Scott made Baltimore the beast of the AFC North in 2008. The offense was still not overpowering, but the Ravens began scoring more points late in the season as rookie quarterback Joe Flacco showed veteran-like poise.

After Baltimore's 11–5 record secured a Wild Card spot in the playoffs, the Ravens made a run at another Super Bowl. First they squashed the Dolphins, 27–9; then they knocked out the top-seeded Titans, 13–10. But there would be no third straight road victory. Facing the Steelers in a hard-hitting AFC Championship Game, Flacco tossed three interceptions, and Baltimore lost 23–14. Still, Coach Harbaugh loved his players'

WILLIS McGAHEE TOPPED 1,000 RUSHING YARDS 4 TIMES IN HIS NFL CAREER

Jamal Lewis

RUNNING BACK / RAVENS SEASONS: 2000–06 / HEIGHT: 5-FOOT-11 / WEIGHT: 245 POUNDS

Jamal Lewis was a freakish running back. At a stocky, bull-necked 245 pounds, he had the ability to blast his way through defenders like a battering ram. Yet he was also amazingly light on his feet, able to dance around linebackers and then outrun defensive backs. During his seven seasons in a Ravens uniform, Lewis experienced the highest of highs and the lowest of lows. He helped Baltimore win the Super Bowl as a rookie in 2000, then tore a knee ligament in training camp the next year and missed the entire 2001 season. Back to form by 2003, he galloped into NFL history with an incredible 2,066-yard rushing effort (including one game with 295 rushing yards, then a league record). A year later, Lewis made headlines of the wrong kind, as he was charged with drug trafficking and sentenced to four months in prison—a term he served before the start of the 2005 season. The Ravens, looking to try a new offensive approach, let Lewis leave town after the 2006 season. He then signed with the rival Cleveland Browns, who had re-entered the league in 1999.

effort. "I couldn't be more proud to stand with them in victory and, today, in defeat," he said.

Harbaugh stood proudly with his scrappy Ravens during a 9–7 season in 2009 as well. Flacco threw for 3,613 yards and 21 touchdowns, and running back Ray Rice tallied 1,339 yards and 7 touchdowns—but it was the defense that saved the day in several close games throughout the season. Not only were the Ravens stingy about giving up points to opponents (their 16.3 points-per-game average was third best in the NFL), but they also helped the offense by forcing 32 total turnovers throughout the season—including a team-record six in a late-season 31–7 rout of the Chicago Bears.

Although the Ravens

TODD HEAP MADE TOUGH CATCHES ACROSS THE MIDDLE OF THE FIELD

ended the season behind the Cincinnati Bengals in the AFC North, they once again earned the Wild Card berth in the playoffs. And once again, Baltimore started out strong in the postseason. In the first round, the Ravens scored 24 points in the first quarter against the powerhouse New England Patriots. Timely interceptions by Reed and cornerback Chris Carr in the second half stifled the Patriots' comeback attempts as the Ravens cruised to a 33–14 victory. But in the second round, it was Baltimore that was restrained. The Colts allowed the Ravens to score only once—a 25-yard field goal by kicker Billy Cundiff—in a 20–3 rout.

The Ravens returned as one of the best teams in the league in 2010 and enjoyed their most successful season since 2006. The addition of brawny wide receiver Anquan Boldin gave Flacco a sure-handed target down the field. The two connected 64 times in 2010, and 7 of the 25 touchdowns Flacco threw landed in Boldin's arms. Lewis, Suggs, and Reed continued their dominance on defense, helping the team tally 19 interceptions and 15 forced fumbles.

As impressive as Baltimore's 12–4 record was, it still was good enough for only second place in the division. The Ravens rode into the playoffs as the Wild Card team and trounced the Chiefs 30–7 in the first round. Then they met up with the rival Steelers in the divisional round. At halftime, the Ravens appeared to have the game in control with a score of 21–7. But then an unfortunate spate of Baltimore

Bitter Rivals

Whether it's a regular-season game or a postseason matchup, every meeting between the Baltimore Ravens and the Pittsburgh Steelers turns into a bitter battle. The two AFC North teams have developed such a fierce rivalry that *Sports Illustrated* ranked it second among the rivalries in the NFL. Although the close proximity of Baltimore and Pittsburgh plays a role in the rivalry, perhaps a bigger factor is the emphasis that both teams place on defense and the pride they take in stifling the opposing offense. The fact that the Steelers have eliminated the Ravens from the postseason three times in recent years has helped fuel the fire as well. On-field arguments between players have happened almost every time the two teams have played. Often, that bad blood carries over into the media as well. "The coaches hate each other, the players hate each other," explained Pittsburgh wide receiver Hines Ward. "There's no calling each other after the game and inviting each other out to dinner. The feeling's mutual: They don't like us, and we don't like them. There's no need to hide it—they know it, and we know it."

THE CITIES OF PITTSBURGH AND BALTIMORE ARE ONLY ABOUT 200 MILES APART

STANDING 5-FOOT-8, RUNNING BACK RAY RICE WAS A SMALL POWERHOUSE

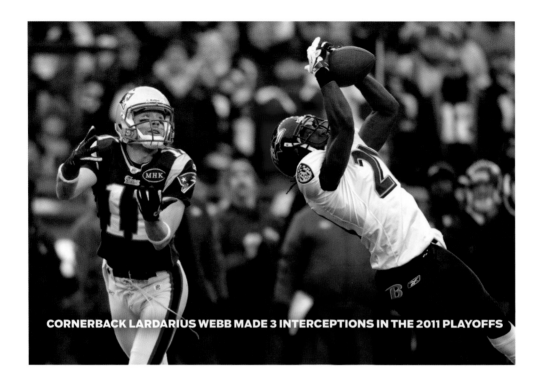

CORNERBACK LARDARIUS WEBB MADE 3 INTERCEPTIONS IN THE 2011 PLAYOFFS

turnovers provided Pittsburgh with the opportunity to tie it up. The Steelers took the lead on a field goal and then sealed their 31–24 victory with a touchdown in the waning moments of the game. "We felt good at the half," Rice said afterwards. "Our defense had them stopped, and I thought we were going to come out and handle our business. But then the situation happened—fumble, turnover, another turnover."

fter stewing over that loss during the long off-season, the Ravens started 2011 with a rematch against the Steelers at M&T Bank Stadium in Baltimore. This time, the Ravens were determined to protect both the ball and the 21–7 lead they had built up by the end of the second quarter. Ngata led a defensive attack that forced seven turnovers, including three in the second half, and paved the way for a 35–7 rout of the Steelers.

That convincing win imbued the Ravens with a sense of confidence that carried them to the top of the AFC North throughout most of the 2011 season. The emergence of tight end Ed Dickson on offense, coupled with Ngata's dominance on defense, helped the Ravens win 12 games, including their first-ever Thanksgiving Day game. "We expect it to be a tight race," Coach Harbaugh said in December. "We just want to uphold our end of the bargain." If it hadn't been for a missed field goal in the final minute of the AFC Championship Game against the Patriots, the Ravens' bargain would have included a trip to the Super Bowl in February 2012.

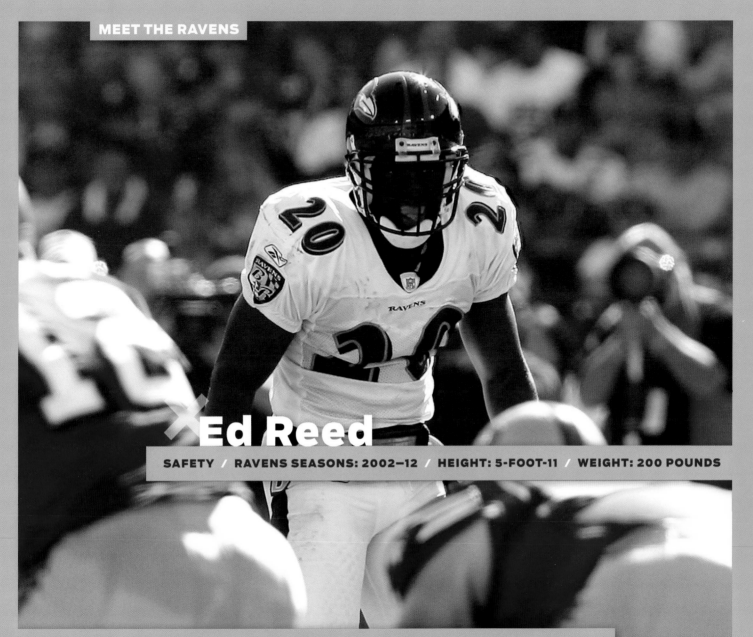

Ed Reed

SAFETY / RAVENS SEASONS: 2002–12 / HEIGHT: 5-FOOT-11 / WEIGHT: 200 POUNDS

Like Ray Lewis, Ed Reed played college football at the University of Miami. And although he was smaller and quieter than Lewis, he played with the same swagger and toughness. After being selected with the 24th overall pick in the 2002 NFL Draft, Reed started every game his rookie season. Naturally fast and fearless, he was also an intelligent player who sought a mental edge by studying game film to learn his opponents' tendencies. The star safety could do it all. In 2002, he blocked the first two punts in Ravens history, returning one for a touchdown. In 2004, he picked off an NFL-high 9 passes and returned one of them 106 yards for a touchdown—the longest scoring play in NFL history at the time. Such efforts cemented his status as, arguably, the game's best safety and earned him the 2004 NFL Defensive Player of the Year award. Still, Reed insisted he could get better. "I have a lot more to learn," he said. "Just like any other thing in life, you want to continue being a student at whatever it is you do."

TORREY SMITH WAS A RISING STAR AFTER A SEVEN-TOUCHDOWN ROOKIE SEASON

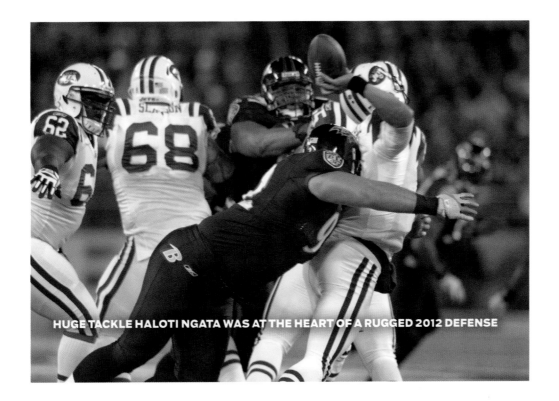

HUGE TACKLE HALOTI NGATA WAS AT THE HEART OF A RUGGED 2012 DEFENSE

One year later, the Ravens got their wish, appearing in Super Bowl XLVII opposite Coach Harbaugh's brother Jim and his San Francisco 49ers. Baltimore went 10–6 in the regular season and captured the AFC championship to wind up in New Orleans in the so-called "Harbaugh Bowl," a contest that featured the longest kickoff return in Super Bowl history (by Ravens defensive tackle Arthur Jones) and a power outage in the midst of the third quarter that delayed the game for 34 minutes. After the lights came back on, the 49ers experienced a surge as well, narrowing the scoring gap but coming up short of Baltimore's stalwart defensive line. The 34–31 Baltimore victory garnered Flacco Super Bowl MVP honors, but much attention was focused on the sole remaining member of the original Ravens squad, Ray Lewis, who was retiring at game's end. "One man can't win a ring," Lewis said, giving credit to teammates such as Reed and Suggs. "It takes a whole team to win a ring."

Exciting seasons have always been part of the deal for Baltimore Ravens fans. In their short history, the Ravens have already appeared in the playoffs multiple times, established one of the most dominating defenses in the history of the league, and brought two Super Bowl trophies home for their fans. Now those fans are eagerly awaiting the day when their favorite purple-and-black-clad team will soar to the Super Bowl once again.

INDEX